How Do Organisms and Their Environments Form an Ecosystem?

 HOUGHTON MIFFLIN HARCOURT

Printed in U.S.A.

ISBN: 978-0-544-07356-2

5 6 7 8 9 10 1083 21 20 19 18 17 16 15 14

4500470080   A B C D E F G

Be an Active Reader!

Look at these words.

environment	photosynthesis	decomposer
ecosystem	producer	food web
habitat	consumer	succession
niche	food chain	extinction

Look for answers to these questions.

Where do organisms live?

Which living things make up an ecosystem?

How do plants get energy to live?

How does energy move in an ecosystem?

How does energy move in a food web?

How can environmental changes affect organisms?

How does an ecosystem go through succession?

How can environmental changes help or hurt an ecosystem?

How do invasive species affect an ecosystem?

What happens to some organisms on Earth?

Where do organisms live?

A forest can be a world of its own, inhabited by a variety of plants and animals. Birds nest in the trees, squirrels look for nuts, and plants use the soil to grow.

An environment is all the living and nonliving things that surround and affect an organism. The soil, water, rocks, light, nutrients, and air make up the nonliving parts of an environment. These nonliving parts are called abiotic parts. The living parts of an environment are called biotic parts.

An environment and all the organisms living in it are called an ecosystem. A forest is just one of the many ecosystems on Earth.

The temperature, weather, and water in a forest affect the organisms that live there.

Which living things make up an ecosystem?

If you look closely at the forest ecosystem, you will notice different groups of living things. You may notice many blue jays, oak trees, and deer. There may be raccoons, owls, and dozens of different types of insects. A group of organisms of the same species in an ecosystem is called a population. All of the maple trees in a single forest make up a population. All of the earthworms in the forest also make up a population.

All organisms in an ecosystem depend on other organisms. An ecosystem that has many populations is diverse. A diverse ecosystem has more resources available to organisms. Most of Earth's diverse ecosystems lie close to the equator. The farther away from the equator an ecosystem is, the less diverse it tends to be.

All of the plant and animal populations that live and interact with one another in an ecosystem are called a community. Many animals in a particular community compete for the same foods. The community outside your schoolyard is part of an ecosystem. The populations of people, plants, and animals make up the community.

Organisms can survive only where their needs are met. A habitat is a place where an organism lives within an ecosystem. Without a habitat, an organism would not have the resources it needs to live. For example, prairie dogs must live in grassland areas.

A niche is an organism's complete role, or function, in its ecosystem. A niche includes the kinds of foods the organism eats, the climate it needs, and even the way the organism obtains and eats its food. Because organisms have their own niche, they can share the same habitat. However, if organisms share a niche in an ecosystem, they have to compete for the same resources.

A niche can be narrow or broad. Animals that eat only a small number of specific foods have a narrow niche. Animals with a broad niche can eat a wide variety of food.

The larva, or caterpillar, of the monarch butterfly eats only milkweed, so the caterpillar has a very narrow niche.

How do plants get energy to live?

Animals get their energy from eating other organisms in their ecosystem. Very few plants can dine on other organisms. Plants need to make their own food in order to get the energy they need to survive. Plants make their own food through a process called photosynthesis. A few things are needed for photosynthesis to occur—water, sunlight, and a gas called carbon dioxide. Water from soil is taken into the plant's roots, and carbon dioxide enters tiny holes in the plant's leaves. Chlorophyll is a green pigment in plants that allows a plant cell to absorb light to make food. The energy from sunlight changes the water and carbon dioxide into sugar and a gas called oxygen. The sugar is used as the plant's food, and the oxygen is released into the air as waste.

sunlight

During photosynthesis, carbon dioxide enters a plant, and oxygen leaves the plant.

oxygen

carbon dioxide

water

Oxygen is a waste product for plants, but it is not waste for animals. In fact, animals need oxygen to live. The carbon dioxide–oxygen cycle is a natural cycle in Earth's atmosphere.

Plants use carbon dioxide and give off oxygen. How does that carbon dioxide get into the air? The gas that one organism needs to take in from the air is the same gas that another organism gives off as a waste product. Plants take in carbon dioxide from the air and give off oxygen as waste. Animals breathe in oxygen from the air, and then they exhale and give off carbon dioxide. Because of this cycle, plants and animals in an ecosystem depend on each other.

All of the plants and animals in an ecosystem are part of the carbon dioxide–oxygen cycle.

How does energy move in an ecosystem?

When plants get energy from sunlight, it is the beginning of a long chain of energy movement in an ecosystem. A plant is called a producer because it makes, or produces, its own food. Each animal in an ecosystem is called a consumer. Consumers get energy from eating, or consuming, other living things. Consumers that eat only plants are called herbivores. Those that eat only animals are called carnivores. Consumers that eat both plants and animals are known as omnivores.

Energy is transferred from sunlight to plants and then to animals. The transfer of food energy between organisms in an ecosystem is called a food chain. A food chain shows the order in which energy flows. All food chains start with the sun and pass energy to a producer and then to a line of consumers.

sun

producer

first-level consumer

second-level consumer

third-level consumer

In a food chain, energy flows from producer to consumer.

Fungi are one kind of decomposer. Like bacteria and certain kinds of worms, they return nutrients to soil.

For example, grasses grow, using sunlight to produce food. When a rabbit eats the grasses, some of the energy flows to the rabbit, called a first-level consumer. Soon a fox comes along and eats the rabbit. This causes the energy to move to the fox, a second-level consumer. Next in the food chain is a golden eagle. As the eagle eats the fox, the energy is passed on again. The golden eagle is a third-level consumer.

At the end of a food chain is the decomposer, which "recycles" dead organisms. A decomposer breaks down the remains of dead organisms so that nutrients from the organisms are returned to the soil. Bacteria and fungi are examples of decomposers. In the food chain described here, bacteria will break down the animals' remains.

How does energy move in a food web?

You can see how energy moves from the rabbit to the snake to the hawk. However, this is not the only way that animals in an ecosystem eat. The rabbit eats a variety of plants, and the snake and hawk eat many types of animals. A group of food chains that overlap is called a food web. Every ecosystem has food chains and food webs.

What if one of the organisms in the web is removed? The other organisms are affected. If the snake is removed from the food web, the rabbit, plant, and hawk populations would be affected.

This food web shows how energy flows from one organism to the next and how the organisms depend on each other.

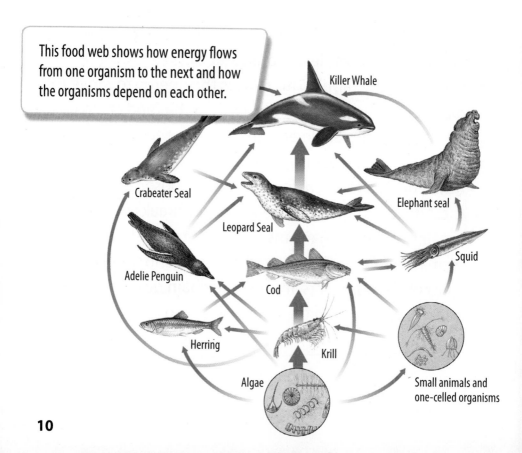

Killer Whale

Crabeater Seal

Leopard Seal

Elephant seal

Squid

Adelie Penguin

Cod

Herring

Krill

Algae

Small animals and one-celled organisms

Without snakes to eat them, more rabbits would survive and eat more plants. Without snakes to eat, the hawks may not find enough food to stay alive.

An energy pyramid is a diagram that shows that energy is lost at each level in a food chain. Organisms store only a small amount of energy from the food they eat. As a result, only a small amount of energy is passed on in the food web. When an animal eats an organism, 90% of the energy is used to keep the animal alive. Only 10% can be passed to whatever organism later eats that animal.

The organisms lower on the pyramid have the greatest amount of energy available to them. Producers have the energy of sunlight to grow. They are the base of the pyramid. The first-level consumers must eat many plants in order to get enough energy to live. As you continue up the energy pyramid, less energy is passed to the higher-level consumers.

The wolf at the top of the pyramid has the least amount of the sun's energy available to it.

How can environmental changes affect organisms?

Environments are changing all the time. Some changes occur slowly over a long period of time. Erosion, the process of moving Earth materials from one place to another, is one kind of slow change. For example, the erosion of rock in a mountaintop takes place slowly as wind wears the rock away.

Erosion can affect the organisms that live on the mountain. The plants have a smaller area to grow in, and the animals have a smaller area in which to move around and look for food. In order to survive, the organisms must make changes or be able to relocate to a new environment. The organisms will die if they cannot adapt, or change, with the environment.

Because erosion changes the surface of a mountaintop, it changes the habitats of plants and animals that live there.

The organisms in the path of a mudslide are affected directly, and the rest of the ecosystem is affected indirectly by the rapid change.

Some changes happen so quickly that there's no time for organisms to adapt to them. For example, floods may occur when rain falls faster than it can soak into the ground. Many plants cannot survive such a rapid change.

Mudslides are fast changes. Soil, rocks, and even trees may slide from a higher area to a lower area. Thousands of organisms may be in the way of this heavy debris. Even organisms that are not in the mudslide's path may be affected by the quick change in the ecosystem, because they may have trouble adapting to the change in food supply.

How does an ecosystem go through succession?

Ecosystems can recover after big changes. Succession is a gradual change in the kinds of organisms in an ecosystem. Succession may occur after a fast change, such as a volcanic eruption. The entire ground may be covered in ash, and often nothing but bare rock is left. Succession that starts from bare rock just after an environmental change is called primary succession.

Tiny organisms such as moss or lichen may grow on the rock. Over time, soil forms after the rock breaks down. Plants grow in the soil. Small animals come to feed on these new plants. When the plants die and decay, they add nutrients to the soil. Over generations, bushes grow, larger animals come to live in the area, and trees finally take root and grow.

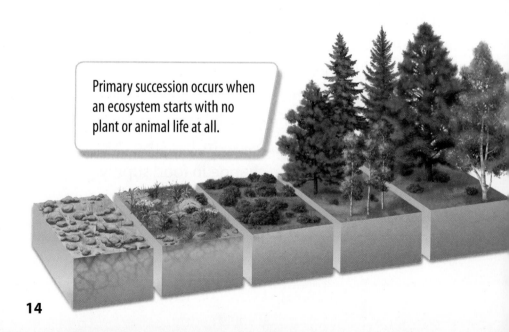

Primary succession occurs when an ecosystem starts with no plant or animal life at all.

Not all changes to an ecosystem destroy the soil like a volcano does. Forest fires can cause drastic changes in an ecosystem, but the soil is still present. Succession that starts from soil is called secondary succession. This kind of succession is faster than primary succession, because there is no need for soil to be made. Seeds and roots grow in the soil after the fire. Plants such as shrubs and grass grow and become food sources for many other living things. Larger plants then take hold in the area, and the new ecosystem becomes dense with life.

In a secondary succession, trees can reappear after a forest fire, and the community becomes reestablished.

How can environmental changes help or hurt an ecosystem?

Not all forest fires destroy an ecosystem. Although some plants and animals may be destroyed, some forest fires can be helpful to the organisms that live in the forest. Most forest fires are started by lightning strikes. The heat from the fire causes the pine cones high in trees to open up and release the seeds inside. The seeds then fall to the ground and grow.

Forest fires might also help to reduce the number of harmful insects, as well as prevent too many large trees from blocking out sunlight and space for other plants. An occasional forest fire can actually help to maintain a forest and its communities.

Some environmental changes can be so harmful that an ecosystem may not be able to recover. This is often the case when changes in climate are involved.

A fire may be harmful to many of the plants and trees, but there are also many benefits to the forest as a whole ecosystem.

The photos show the difference between a coral environment that has been damaged by coral bleaching and one that is healthy.

A coral reef is an important ocean ecosystem in tropical areas. Coral is made of tiny organisms called polyps, and these polyps grow, spread, and connect to form a coral reef. Fish and other organisms depend on the reef for shelter and an area to find food.

Algae live in the coral. They provide food to the coral and give the coral its diverse colors. Some coral reefs are being damaged by changes in water temperature. When the water gets too warm or too cold, the coral expel the algae. Without the algae, the coral looks white, or bleached. When a population that so many other organisms depend on is damaged, the entire ecosystem is affected.

How do invasive species affect an ecosystem?

Most animals have natural predators that keep their population from getting too large. But what happens when a species from another place is introduced to an ecosystem?

An invasive species is one that invades, or takes over, a place because the species has no natural predators there. Invasive species compete to survive in the new ecosystem, and they often win. They take the food supply from native species in the area.

Kudzu is a plant native to Asia. It was introduced in the United States to help control soil erosion, but it competes for space with all of the other plants around it.

Invasive plants crowd out other plants. The invasive plants may reproduce quickly and spread over a large area. Once an invasive species takes hold in an ecosystem, the species can reduce or destroy the populations of native species.

How are invasive species introduced to ecosystems? People may put a plant from another area of the world into their garden. They may let a pet or other animal loose into a new environment. Even birds can introduce invasive species by carrying plant seeds to new places.

An invasive species has been damaging the ecosystem of Yellowstone National Park. A lake trout that was introduced to the area has been slowly taking over the ecosystem. This trout is competing with other fish and organisms, especially the Yellowstone cutthroat trout, which is endangered, or close to dying out. The lake trout has no natural predators in the Yellowstone ecosystem, so its population has been growing quickly. Scientists are finding it challenging to help the ecosystem return to balance.

The invasive lake trout is competing for resources with the endangered Yellowstone cutthroat trout.

What happens to some organisms on Earth?

Some effects of ecosystem changes are permanent. Extinction occurs when a species of plant or animal is no longer living, or existing, anywhere on Earth. Extinction can happen for many reasons. The organism may become unable to compete for resources, and it may simply die off faster than it can reproduce. Humans can play a role in the extinction of some animals by hunting, fishing, and destroying habitats.

The passenger pigeon became extinct in 1914. This extinction was the result of excessive hunting by humans.

Natural changes to ecosystems, such as massive volcanic eruptions and large asteroid impacts, can also cause extinctions. Scientists have evidence that such events in Earth's history caused many species to become extinct in a short amount of time.

People can take action to prevent species from becoming extinct. Scientists can educate people to make them aware of plants and animals that are endangered and could become extinct in the future. With this awareness, people can protect the habitats and ecosystems of these organisms.

There are also ways to maintain ecosystems. Limiting the areas where people build and limiting the species that can be hunted or fished are ways of preserving ecosystems.

The relationships that organisms have with their ecosystem can be complex. By learning about these relationships, scientists can determine how to prevent human activity from destroying ecosystems.

The Texas star cactus is an endangered plant species. Loss of habitat and over-harvesting by cactus collectors have threatened its survival in the wild. It is now a protected species in Texas.

Model a Food Web

Choose an ecosystem, and research the different types of interactions between plants and animals in that ecosystem. Make a model of a food web, including as many organisms as you can. Use arrows to connect the pictures or models of each plant or animal.

Write a Letter

Write a letter to a local newspaper or government official to explain the importance of protecting ecosystems and the organisms that live in those ecosystems. The letter should include ways that people can help ecosystems and the consequences of not protecting ecosystems.

Glossary

consumer [kuhn·SOOM·er] A living thing that cannot make its own food and must eat other living things.

decomposer [dee·kuhm·POH·ser] A living thing that gets energy by breaking down dead organisms and animal wastes into simpler substances.

ecosystem [EE·koh·sis·tuhm] A community of organisms and the environment in which they live.

environment [en·VY·ruhn·muhnt] All the living and nonliving things that surround and affect an organism.

extinction [ek·STINGK·shuhn] A plant or an animal species that is no longer living or existing.

food chain [FOOD CHAYN] The transfer of food energy between organisms in an ecosystem.

food web [FOOD WEB] A group of food chains that overlap.

habitat [HAB·i·tat] The place where an organism lives and can find everything it needs to survive.

niche [NICH] The role a plant or animal plays in its habitat.

photosynthesis [foh·toh·SIN·thuh·sis] The process that plants use to make their own food.

producer [pruh·DOOS·er] A living thing, such as a plant, that can make its own food.

succession [suhk·SESH·uhn] A gradual change of the kinds of organisms in an ecosystem.